The River Where You Forgot My Name

Crab Orchard Series in Poetry
OPEN COMPETITION AWARD

The River Where You Forgot My Name

POEMS BY **CORRIE WILLIAMSON**

Crab Orchard Review &
Southern Illinois University Press
Carbondale

Southern Illinois University Press
www.siupress.com

22 21 20 19   4 3 2 1

The Crab Orchard Series in Poetry is a joint publishing venture of
Southern Illinois University Press and *Crab Orchard Review*. This
series has been made possible by the generous support of the Office
of the President of Southern Illinois University and the Office of
the Vice Chancellor for Academic Affairs and Provost at Southern
Illinois University Carbondale.

Editor of the Crab Orchard Series in Poetry: Jon Tribble
Judge for the 2018 Open Competition Award: Allison Joseph

Cover illustration: "Montana Topographic Map Isolated," by Frank
Ramspott; iStock

Library of Congress Cataloging-in-Publication Data
Names: Williamson, Corrie, author.
Title: The river where you forgot my name : poems / by Corrie
Williamson.
Description: Carbondale : Crab Orchard Review & Southern Illinois
University Press, [2019] | Series: Crab Orchard series in poetry
Identifiers: LCCN 2019002520 | ISBN 9780809337477
(paperback : alk. paper) | ISBN 9780809337484 (e-book)
Subjects: | BISAC: POETRY / American / General.
Classification: LCC PS3623.I5673 A6 2019 | DDC 811/.6—dc23
LC record available at https://lccn.loc.gov/2019002520

Printed on recycled paper. ♻

This paper meets the requirements of ANSI/NISO Z39.48-1992
(Permanence of Paper). ∞

Time is a river that sweeps me along, but I am the river; it is a tiger that mangles me, but I am the tiger; it is a fire that consumes me, but I am the fire.

CONTENTS

The River Where You
Forgot My Name

Hay Cutting

Fincastle, Virginia, 1803

The sky is just as I imagine
an ocean, vast & unmarred
by cloud. I have yet to learn
to walk among the seedheads
knowing with my palms
their story of moisture,
of readiness. The dew
whisked off now into light,
the reapers gather
at the edges of the grass,
having spent the morning
snarling their blades against
grindstones in a flurry
of deadly sparks. They move
together across the rows,
blurring in the heat,
their scythes like a flock of steel
birds released from the field.

I
Montana

52 Hertz
a letter to Shea in Kitty Hawk, North Carolina

No rebellions from the sea of late, you write. You must be pleased to see it calm, the gray Atlantic, which yearly moves the slender strip of your island a little east, a little west. Across the continent the whale known as the loneliest leviathan on earth roams northward to Kodiak & the Aleutians, singing as much to the silver-furred grizzly kings & to the blue spruce as to its own kind. I can hardly stand to think of it—that solitary keen in the ocean's dusk. Too high for anyone to hear but a headphone-clad oceanographer in NOAA's quiet coastal observatory. (That is, you must know, my favorite of all acronyms.) There are those who suggest the 52 hertz whale is deaf. Mostly deaf people have suggested this. (*Dear cetologists: Have you considered the possibility the whale is singing into silence, into a trembling in his own bones?*) Your letter describes a little paper bag full of last year's white poplar leaves, like plaster chiselings. Pelicans ruling thrones of old pilings. A sable horse by the frosted pond. Your cats inspecting the valleys between one another's claws. I'd gather them, if I could, sing in their language. I'll pen this letter on a single olive leaf. I'll tell you what I saw today: flecked sparrows in the winter brush, cobble-eyed, close enough to touch.

The Pleasuring Ground, or This Week in Animal News

The number of "dee" suffixes used at the end of the call denotes the size of the threat.
The more "dees," the bigger the threat. So if you hear the call "chick-a-dee-dee," that
means a smaller threat than if you hear "chick-a-dee-dee-dee-dee." Of course, the
threat level is from the perspective of a chickadee.

In Rajasthan, a camel chews the head off its owner after standing
tied all day in the sun. A gorilla is shot with its huge cartographic

hand encircling a human child's forearm. A bison calf washes
down the Madison, is stuffed shivering in the trunk of a tourist's sedan

& euthanized when its herd does not accept its escape from loss. I find
a note I've written myself: albatross, three-hinged wings, multiple mothers.

Lovely, but I've forgotten where I was headed with it. The black-capped
chickadee has one of the most advanced nonhuman language systems

on earth. Their song can say, I hop on the ground, or I fear from this branch,
denote a threat in the air, or from below, & summon their fellows

to mob. In the original language of our nation's first park & its second-
chance wolves, the land we share is dubbed a pleasuring ground. This year, we

will shoot grizzly bear for sport. The judge in the NYT article condemning
the de-endangerment of the wolverine calls the beast cryptic, old word

for occult, for mysticism worthy of concealing: term for the wishes
of the dead, the tomb where we bury alive the ebbing babble of the wild.

Gates of the Mountains

it[s] note is not disagreeable though loud—
        —Meriwether Lewis, first written description of the magpie

Magpies like the one the Corps
sent back to Monticello
in a cage made of sticks & hide

swoop from crags, their long
black tails flashing emerald
in sunshafts. Dammed all along

its path, the Missouri here
languishes pondlike, still enough
for algae's viscous bloom.

Once through the high banks
the waters cannot help but narrow,
pale cliffs demanding channel,

a thread. Only the wind stirs
the surface, the true current
vanquished, though unlike so many

of his christenings, the name Lewis
gave this place remains—the canyon's
thick shoulders unchanged,

cave-riddled, flanked by palisades
of stone. Perhaps some lost note
is held in echo where the cliffs

fold tightest. But when I call out,
the reply is cold & far-off:
a shout from a distant room,

or the call of a bird awakened
from flight-dream & flock
to solitude, to mist-laden eastern light,

its raspy bark & clattery trill
echoless, & for a thousand miles
the only one of its kind.

The Valley of a Thousand Haystacks

near Garrison

The thin vein of the Little Blackfoot slips among fields dotted with the old beaverslide hay stackers, bony lodgepole skeletons that still creak to work in this valley. Hay is loaded into carts from swept windrows on the open palms of pitchforks. The shoulders of the horses haul the rake through the air, scaffolding shuddering in the autumn light & the fodder falls, released like a rib's caged breath. Let us call this progress: the steady growing of the stack, like dough warm & rising in the field, a bond against cold, hunger, zephyr, rot's black blooms—this banked seed of root & sun. Let us eat that bread in winter's rooms.

At the Farmers Union's Women's Conference in Paradise, Montana

The herbalist has hair like a red horsetail
& I have had too little coffee to stomach
some of the Gaia woo-woo but I am trying

to listen when she speaks about magpies
nesting in the brambling hawthorn.
She is saying Saint John's wort is

community, is the sun, is my mother,
& she actually uses the words *maiden*
& *crone* to describe her audience & tells

us that yarrow root will stop bleeding
but start menstrual flows & all I can think
is that yarrow must be an old word indeed

& weaves together yesterday & tomorrow,
used by Achilles on the battlefields of Troy
to sop his brothers' rosy wounds while

on she goes, this skinny oracle, her
lilt a quiet one but I peg her for a native when
she says *measure*, the long open-mouthed

melodic *may* of the first syllable
catching me again as it did the first time
I heard the lentil farmer use it to describe

the wealth of dirt & knew something
in the tone had traveled from a white
& green country of ice to live here

like a castaway whose black ship sails
a sea of grass, telling me how to measure
the tincture, the root, the loess, while outside

snow is falling on the earthly garden & my brain
stumbles with white flowers & wanting
to say *oh sisters, oh city keepers, yellow sparrows.*

Butte Tango

That one they call
       Orphan Girl, he says, because she's off on her own,
& she is, the old gallows frame
       that lowered miners, mules, their earth-shearing tools
into the ground, & hauled
       up porous loads of storm-&-pond colored ore.
The city, out of pride
       or something like it, outlines the tired frames
in red lights, & we
       are lit up too, tonight, warm from the hot springs
& the wine we pass
       between us in a carton. His hands are very fine,
orchids, root clusters,
       & I like them on the wheel, & taking the wine
from me. There can be
       no danger here, it seems, now or later when his pulse
strikes fast between the blades
       of my back, while far beyond the richest hill
on earth, beyond the divide,
       my mother's heart is slowing after an evening whirl
across the dance floor with my father,
       electrical impulses not quick enough, misfiring,
a broken sheave.
       He's drawn the curtains, but on the slope outside
the window, the gallows frames
       glow red as claret, gazing down into the dim vein
through which they no longer fall.

Vultures: Collective Noun

I've never seen them so clearly ominous—
but what I mean is omen-ous—roosting
on a steel-eyed day, in a dead tree, like a perfect
cliché. A *kettle*, they're called, when circling,
but these are still, which makes them a *venue*.
At least nine, & one of them has spread
his wings to dry against the afternoon's
wet blues. He seems about to launch, or else
the anchor of this gloom. They are silhouette,
hemmed & feathered line. *Everyone on this street
is going to church tomorrow*, he says, as we drive
beneath. I'll go, too, & keep my shoulders still,
eye out my congregation: is it brood, nest,
or congress—a venue for my darkness' unrest?

Hiking to Goldbug Hot Springs, I Consider the Discovery
of Lewis & Clark's Shitter at Travelers' Rest

From September to June, the men shed through their bodies waste
        starred with bright shards of mercury, Lewis's cure-all
drug & the soil's constellated clue to archaeologists.

Across the border in Idaho, I make my way from where the trail
        begins at a wooden outhouse to the spring, which gives
itself away by a stitch of steam in the canyon's side, billow

in waning light into which I lower, float my feet over warm
        beryl stones, thinking of Lewis's account of seeing
the great falls, his lone ecstatics, penstrokes insufficient

to express his joy, his meal that night of buffalo
        marrowbones, which he called *sumptuous*. Those
drifting months, he woke with the dawn

between his teeth. The dirt ate willingly enough the sorrow
        he cast off. My hands ripple in the stream, flesh
unhinging between air & water warmed in a dark kettle

in the ground, above this valley of lupine & tall
        pine, private as a family charnel, recalling the passage
that describes the prairie burning, the child who survives

beneath a green buffalo hide: emerging to shed the skin
        on blistered grass, body come up shining
from the well of heat down which it had been cast.

Bread Alone

Having accidentally thrown out their decade-old sourdough culture,
the bakers at Park Avenue come to my friend Nick at the Sweet
Grass & ask, can he find it in his heart to share a dollop of starter
with them, but though he is kind about it, though he says, ask me
for sugar, for flour, for honey brewed by bees from high mountain
meadows beyond the valley, no, he cannot give them a bit of the
batter that dwells in a plastic bucket by his rusty ovens, birthed 150
years ago in the windy darkness of a kitchen in Great Falls at the
hands of a Scotch sheepherder plying yeast with water, with wheat
that bloomed & died in the surrounding plains, risen from the wild,
the dough a thing with breath, souring into a richness he feeds, &
folds, hungrily alive in his long freckled hands, like the voice
blazing in a coal worn in a bag below the throat, talisman & torch,
the voice that gives the price for day-old bread, the voice vowing
the simple, leavening power of its love, the voice of some god
howling year after year among the trees.

Double Ekphrastic: Charles Willson Peale's "Exhumation
of the Mastodon" & "The Artist in His Museum"

In the first painting, there are no visible bones
save for one in frozen flutter on the banner
that suggests some kind of ideal femur, some

buried prize. Its name is full of its mystery,
mammoth a rough translation for earth-horn,
which Jefferson synonymed with *massive*, while

mastodon comes down through either the farmer,
Masten, from whose earth the earthhorn
first emerged, or a combination of *breast*

& *dentine*, Cuvier's *nipple tooth* coinage
to describe its rippled incisors. Out of the pit,
out of the painting's pool comes *incognitum*,

comes *nephraim*, harbinger of extinction,
prover of man's nature murderous.
The second painting shows him rebuilt,

or mostly, hulking in the nation's first
museum of paleontology. Hush now, all
will be revealed: the great ankles & rootlike

knobbled feet, now the knees, the lower
caging of the ribs, revealing the beast
headlines remind us we'll be de-extincting by

by 2050, loneliest & largest floating furry
embryo in its truck-sized test tube & meanwhile
Peale in self-portrait is lifting, in perpetuity

lifting, open-palmed, the red velvet curtain.

II
Virginia, 1804–1808

Shenandoah, I love your daughter
Look away, you rollin' river.
                    —American folk song

Chestnut Sabbath

Fincastle, 1804

What clamored squall
in startling a tom turkey

back to chestnuts' shelter
from his worm shucking

in the dawn-wet fields,
ritual of snaring &

snipping from their lives
the little soileaters pulled up

like thread from the earth's
stormy needlepoint canvas

to keep from drowning.
He squabbles in shade

now, hunts leaf litter
& de-armors the chestnuts

beneath their mother trees,
watch-keepers aged & aging

in their uninterrupted
dominion. Time is its own

form of idle malady, which
stirs, brews, fruits, or

readies its black powder
beyond our knowing. All

things abide here between
summon & pluck.

Waiting to Ride
Fincastle, 1805

I paddle like a water strider
in the hayloft, gather

wheatheads & the soft,
dense nests of mice. Into

one, I place the weightless
body of a bee pocketed

in the cellar, like a coin
for the eyes of the passing

season. The horses in
their blue paddock of hills

stamp, impatient for the task.
I see only that work arrives

from a place unseen, gathers
like the iron rustle of August

storms, but to where does it
pass? The horses huck their jaws

while the men's saddling
hands in small unthinking

praise dip like oars against
the glossy river of their throats.

Science Lesson
Fincastle, 1805

What a little fool to think the moon
free & unheeled, to assume she visits

of her own volition, dons her dark
tunic & turns her back upon her

particular mood. Of course a larger
force compels her. Silly, silly, to think

she would blithely beam on the markets
of men were she unbound as she seems

even now, through the barred panes,
violet as a turnip in a tin bucket,

but caught there, snared in her
cistern of blue moss & mirrored fire.

Bringing Home the Bull
Fincastle, 1806

He follows, docile furnace
of red hide & horn.
The wheels of his hooves

clobber stones. Father
carries only a bucket,
swinging from his elbow

for the miles he drove
the monster with neither
lead nor hook. What

a trap for a vast heart,
for hot rivers of blood
beneath the twitching

rusty coat, under
the creasing knees &
rolling haunch, the velvet

sack of his underbelly.
Hide is flesh, & also
my first instinct.

But no, I'm no child,
& coursing in me this
need: to come to him

steady, find that heat echoed
in my wrists, between us
all sinew, flame, & thew.

Completion of the Jackson Ferry Shot Tower
Wythe County, 1807

Freefall perfects the form. A fire
roars at the tower's height, turns

lead molten, moon-faced. It slips
through copper sieve, each drop

pulled into sphere by descent
through a limestone column, walls

thicker than a woman's arm
is long. It drops through shadow

above the riverside, bank & cliff
extending the dive, through the hill

& red dirt tunnel below, to land
steaming in the buried kettle. Admire

it now, the polished shine, for it
must journey down again, plummeting

through the breath & blood—
navigate the flesh to seek the skull's

brittle casket, end the fragile hour,
& drag back to earth its native ore.

Field Clearing, after the Wedding
Fincastle, 1808

When trees cast their shadows
in a long line, their gathered shade

brushing the nearest tree's trunk
& branches, they may be cleared

in a single roiling wave. Cuts
must be well placed. The wedged

mouth of the notch determines
direction of fall, heartwood collapsing

against itself upon vacant space
until the hinge tears, & the first tree

goes, forcing down the next,
& the next's deep weight dragging

under its neighbor like drowning men,
all husked & stripped, limbs

like severed things, heart bucked into
pieces inside the flesh's splintered calm.

Hawk Moth

Fincastle, 1808

Your name driftwood
in the throat, cudgeling
the brain. I know
you're no bird: moonlight
sipper, backward flitter,
gnawer of gingham
& clawer of sills. On cool
eves you shudder
to keep warm, beating
out your fragrant
slumber-musk, night
after night into dust.
Meanwhile, your endless
tongue gravely unfurls
into deep-throated
flowers' sweet-scented spurs.

III
Montana

Mastodon

If the Northwest Passage
weren't foolish enough,
Jefferson thought perhaps
the boys, whose guns could
barely bring down Griz
(Lewis noting: *These bear*
being so hard to die rather
intimidate us all: I confess
I do not like the gentlemen),
would find a still-roaming
mastodon. He hungered
for the history of their bones,
would have been so pleased
to take his afternoon nap within
that cavernous cranium, or
better yet, hobble a live
one to a fencepost, for
those sunlit days when he felt
like riding between rows
of sea kale & cabbage,
palming its rusty, foot-long
guard hair (imagining what
a fine rug it would make
in Monticello's entryway)
as he gazed down at the humped
smoke-blue backs of the old
Appalachians, & admired
the turnip-white tusks jutting
out between his stockings.

April & the Iron-Eaters
Berkeley Pit: Butte

Should we call the snow geese foolish
for not having known that the green lake

amidst the yellow rock where the waters
of the nation divide was in fact a pit of poison

more acidic than a can of Coke? Perhaps.
Though let's not blame them, especially the ones

that perished, floated like sacked pillows
on the still surface or sank bottomward

a thousand feet down, toward the gleaming
arsenic, sulfide still sputtering from mineshafts

like a toxic starfield without the light of fusion.
Now, fireworks & loudspeakers warn migrators:

*Move on, there is no birth, no shelter, no solace
here.* Except of course for the extremophiles

repairing in the earth's harsh dark their own
haggard DNA, among them *Euglena mutabilis,*

which pulls ore from the water to store within
its single cell, then belches air. Ghostly

metal-belly, bizarre homemaker, that as it swims
is forging of waste its version of spring.

Love Song of the Barred Owl

with a line from Robinson Jeffers

I know her tune from childhood twilights,
a question out of shadows—*who cooks
for you? who cooks for y'all?*—falling
through the dusk-washed leaves. Odd
query from a beast that swallows her prey
headfirst & whole. Tonight, she startles
me from high up in the hickory,
with a strange new call—the *hoo-aw,*
screech chased by a gurgle, knife & water
paired. She's courting one I cannot see,
the sails of his wings folded in some hidden
place against the birchbark patterns
of his stout body. Perhaps she has prepared
the nest already: an old woodpecker's
hollow, laid with snipped cedar sprigs
& green-gray flakes of lichen. Wailing
now again in the branches, she summons
him to her need: all fierce, all flesheater.

Ode to the Come-Along

Crablike, with an exoskeleton
of iron, you're elbow,
crank & tooth. Unspooling
the chainlink
choker, I drape a necklace
around the smooth
gray throat of maple,
as anchor, loop
cable around & around
the rhododendron's
bulbous stump.

Overhead, bees
thrum in the white
clusters of laurel
flower; their cousins,
the hornets, tend
to the nearby hive
hanging like a raindrop
turned to pale pulp,
delicate shape belying
the hard geometry
of cells inside. To each
her own work.

When I tug the ratchet,
you rise, dance, wheel & tine
clicking, steel cord
straining against roots,
which have but one
wish—to remain, & claw
the soil like tendon
beginning to crack,
& pop, & snarl, as I
crank, & crank,

praying to the rigid
god that your cable
holds, praying for steel
to outdo seed, this
once—& there, the roots
bared in the shape
of their seeking.

Know You from Adam

A blessing for J. & E., awaiting the birth of their first child

Charming, conjurous, but never an expression
I set stock in. Couldn't I spot him

in a crowd, after all? The autumnally red
hair with its perpetual cargo of twig & leaf,

the tawny skin, his shirtsleeves rolled high
& his twill pants tucked up around his ankles

like a bicyclist. His eyes would have a far-off
look. He'd speak soft, with the confidence

of one long accustomed to gazing into the sub-
terranean sense of things, & summoning the word.

But thinking of you in these slow days
before the birth, my wish for you

is that the old adage ring true, & the babe
not know you from Adam. That borne

through the little yard in Pittsburgh
as you point to raspberries & kale, to the fall's

last lavender sprigs & the changing oak leaves
lining the street, to him you will be the right, pure

giver of all appellation, & the child himself
like the rivers of that city, Allegheny, Ohio,

Monongahela, braiding their ancient tendons
under bridges of steel, carrying over

all they touch, through darkness, against stone,
dam & drought, the gasping weight of a name.

Endless Forms Most Beautiful

He is lying, oh my best beloved, on the floor, reading aloud
from my grandmother's copy of the *Just So Stories*, & his
voice feels out & grows full with the tones of Suleiman-bin-
Daoud & the Most Beautiful & Splendid Balkis whose
cleverness trumps them all. He is the king, the many wives,
& the butterfly who stamps & makes the palace crumble.

For years I prayed that I would not inherit my grandmother's
orchids, those ancient fireworks of temptation, sex embalmed
in the name itself, freckle & bulbous-throated bloom
beckoning even as they burst from jars in the angled light of
her stony greenhouse. Their faces bear a symmetry like ours.
They demand hours tending their luring seams, repotting the
testicular roots. Masquerader, dinosaur, perfumed mutants,
wild caprice beloved of Darwin, who said it would have been
monstrous to imagine an orchid created as we see it now, as
if a god capable of forming from nothing those shapely folds
& flushed flesh could only have been fashioned by the lean
darkness of years, conceiving of neither modesty nor death.

The butterfly sees a higher frequency than we can hope for, a
violet, unimaginable depth woven into mosaic by its many
eyes. Imagine a plant plain as the common pea. What chaos
& gleam the butterfly would see, never so beautiful except
perhaps to the old monk himself, in the monastery's stone-
walled garden, robed knees making half-moons in the soil,
light flaring off spectacles & the chalk-smooth leaves of the
pea plants, which he bends closer to view, the flowers'
precious color, oh, oh my best beloved, opening.

In the Divorce, Patricia Got the Mammoth Bone

She takes it from
the mantel: ulna,
skeletal wedge
mapped with hairline
cracks, & offers
me the bare
billow of its weight,
creeklike scrapes
in the bone where
Alaskan ground squirrels
gnawed toward
the marrow.
We run our palms
over it, consider
setting our teeth
to its edge, imagine
scavengers scattering
when along came
something bigger.
Hunger's warm
rhythm is here in
the white scar
of seeking, of fang
on bone our fingers
trace, ghost-tonguing
this path, this past,
its precious fracture.

Strange Things the Animals Do

When she is ripe with the worker bees' royal jelly the queen newly hatched from her waxcapped queen cup shivers in the hive & dances & drums her feet until the other nascent-but-not-to-be queens emerge & she one by one stings them to death. The hunted are the hardiest learners & in places where coon dogs yowling hunt the masked one, the largest & cleverest of the midnight-eyeshiners, the weird-handed hunchedbacks, learn to lure the canines to the deep parts of the river, clamber their way headward, grip the ears with tarry clawed palms & ride their weight water-down until the dogs are drowned. A female porcupine lays her own tail down her back, prickle to prickle, the tail's bared underside a landing pad for her mate, protecting him from her spiny self with her self so that she may conceive & when her porcupette arrives, listen for her song, a mumbling, sweet hum, as she sits suckling. The grizzlies in the land of the Weathermaker sometimes wake in winter & go walking about as ice collects in their dense hair, a shimmering frost-armor that shakes & crackles like fire in the cold & pokes them as they lie sleeping upon the claimed dead which they will rise & eat. When walking within groves I think of your body, how the sinewy branch of this bristlecone pine (which may live for five thousand years & the most ancient of which was cut down by a budding dendrochronologist who jammed his borer in the dense wood & wanted it back & to chop down is easier than to extract with slow finesse & thus died the oldest known nonclonal organism on earth) reminds me of the dimpled pit of your raised arm & that I would like to nestle my nose there in its opossum's nest blossom of hair, startle you from sleep, & withdraw, quick & furtive as the African greater honeyguide who whistles *tya, tya, brrr-hm* when she is ready to lead the locals to a hive, flashing gold shoulders as she hops ahead & he unsheathes the sweet with his machete, gathers the honey amid the righteous whirring bees, & leaves for the guide larva, wax, &, yes, a dollop of honey, a nod, a thanks, lest next time she calls she leads him to lions.

Winter in Montana: Lewis's List

> *... if it's very important, it's very short. If it's not important, it's very long.*
> *That's a rule in almost all texts.*
>
> —Karl Ove Knausgaard

Lewis's list of expedition supplies goes on for pages that begin with *2 Hadley's Quadrants* (for finding the height of sun or star above horizon) & end with eight nests of camp kettles (*brass is much preferr'd to Iron*). I like to think of him like this, his desk in the swamp of DC, capitol roof half constructed, horseflies clobbering the rafters while he sought to imagine a western winter & all the tools & trinkets that would get him through it, though he could not of course get his brain around such a thing while hunkered in the rolling bowl of the Appalachians, bellied soft & low by the centuries. In his company came the first fiddle to sing in the Rockies, wood shrunk tight as a fish's scale-coat, spurring dancing while the temperature lurked at forty below. *A cheap portable microscope,* he listed, as if Secretary Dearborn might pick one up on his next trip to the District Walmart. *Creyons. 500 best Flints. 15 woolen overalls. 30 shirts of Strong linnen.* The lakes are freezing, trees spearing the snow with their shadows, & lurking in my brain is that lurch across the continent, first wave of death for those who needed no sextant or chronometer. *2 Vials of Phosforus. 24 Iron Spoons. 1 Sea Grass Hammock. 6 Kegs of 5 Gallons each for making 30 Gallons of rectified spirits such as is used for the Indian trade.* Yet he loved those days beyond adventure, beyond compass needle & parallax, never knowing himself better than when he took a blade to a frostbitten toe by starlight. *1 Iron frame Canoe 40 feet long* (that sucker sank). *12 oz Opium.* & the absurd *instrument for measuring made of tape with feet & inches mark'd on it, confined within a circular lethern box of sufficient thickness to admit the width of the tape which has one of its ends confined to an axis of metal passing through the center of the box, around which & within the box it is readily wound by means of a small crank on the outer side of the box which forms a part of the axis, the tape when necessary is drawn out with the same facility & ease with which it is wound up,* which is quite a way to say, don't forget the measuring tape, because I guess no one had bothered to name the fucking thing yet but he was sure of its necessity. The mandate seemed so simple, after all, the goal direct: pass into wildness, measure, & make account.

IV
Saint Louis, Missouri,
1808–1818

After the return of the Corps of Discovery, Clark wasted little time in
finding himself a wife. His bride-to-be, then-sixteen-year-old Julia
Hancock, of Fincastle, Virginia, had caught his eye when she was
a child before Clark went west. Clark wrote to Lewis in 1808,
"I have discovered a most lovely girl Butiful rich possessing
those accomplishments which is calculated to make a
man happy—inferior to you—but to few others."

A Tour of the Elm Street Office of the *Missouri Gazette*,
the First Paper Published West of the Mississippi
Saint Louis, 1808

> It is self-evident that in every country where the rays of the Press is not
> clouded by despotic power ... there science holds her head erect, and
> bids her sons to call into action those talents which lie in a good soil
> inviting cultivation. The inviolation of the Press is co-existent with the
> liberties of the people, they live or die together, it is the vestal fire upon
> the preservation of which, the fate of the nation depends.
>
> —Missouri Gazette *prospectus*

Our arrival precedes the news
by just a month. Come July, the press'

ink runs wet & laps the thick foolscap
curling to meet it in the humid

air, the pretty Ramage rigged a little
like a guillotine but patting with praise

of her own prospectus. It's well
enough, given the weeks of wait

for papers with word of the East,
given the drowning of the postrider

carrying money to convince
the publisher to come to us & print

our laws, else how could we abide
them? Our doings & our dyings, our

disdain for one another squeeze
into a pair of columns, our small

justices, our poems & parties lined
up letter by letter neat as clay

cut into bricks & stacked to dry,
or the tombs in the charnel

with their winged death's heads
& cherubs, their willows drooping

like perfect letterpressed *W*'s
& *M*'s any of which might cry

welcome, comfort, warmth or may
yet spell *welter, malady, war.*

On the Death of Meriwether Lewis

Saint Louis, 1809

> *I fear O! I fear the waight of his mind has over come him,*
> *what will be the Consequence? what will become of ~~my~~ his papers?*
> —William Clark, letter to his brother

The newspaper roared he'd slit his throat. You
believed at first, though it was a horse pistol's
three bullets flaring like a tuning fiddle squall.

You mourn him more than most, but my mind
returns daily to the dog, the steadying breath
of him, his weight like fast water against the legs.

Cold master, to leave the one who followed
him farther than the mind can muster muzzling
out stillness & the brickish smell of blood

shipwrecked by fidelity. What comes in the wake
for our firstborn carrying the dead one's name
like a wet burlap sack, name I have written over

& over into a fineness of ink that feels it must
go on without cease? What beyond the striking
through of the body becomes of a bond?

The River Where You Forgot My Name

Saint Louis, 1810

> *I thank providence for directing the whale to us; & think Him much*
> *more kind to us than he was to Jonah, having Sent this monster to be*
> *Swallowed by us in Sted of Swallowing of us as jonah's did.*
>
> —William Clark, January 10, 1805, journal entry

The curved breast
of the carcass like a ship,
its great beaked head
beached. You arrived
too late for harvesting
much, a bit of blubber
to season with salt
boiled on the cragged,
fog-shucked shore,
& a splash of oil, lighting
a few wet nights. Into
the darkness where
the beast was born
flows the river where you
forgot my name, gifting
it to the girl only a father
ever summoned as *Judith*.
Forgivable, like most sins
of omission, for a man
who knew only
the obedient child, the one
trying now to swallow
the vastness of it: memory's
cold sinew, western sky,
whale, the will of a lord
who strands what he made.

Unrest: Addressing the Great Comet
Saint Louis, 1811

What vast hickory in the sky
are you smoothing with that blade?

You swing against the night
like papa's adze, sweet

for making logs sleek to keep out
rot & ice. This house is sturdy

enough, his shoulders
wide & freckled like the stars

you hide. Perhaps you are the bear's
heart, burning there. You fall

as if to auger the earth,
which shakes already, & tears, night

bristling with the beauty of axes
raised high above men's skulls.

Leap Year & the New Madrid Earthquakes
Saint Louis, 1812

In town, chimneys fall
like wasps' nests

broomed from eaves.
The bricked streets chasm

into maws. Bells rang
as far away as Boston,

the papers claim, whole
forests dragged into

fissures, the big muddy
calved & stalling around

newborn islands, riverboats
adrift like hickory leaves

on the backwards current.
Some say Tecumseh has put

his foot down, & who
could blame him. But I ask

if it may be only the earth
straining to snare her trail,

that promised, unending
orb she must keep, wobbling

as she goes, covetous
yet of the light's sure leap.

Lullaby for Jean Baptiste
Saint Louis, 1813

My bounty is as boundless
as the sea, my love as deep;

the more I give to thee
the more I have, for both

are infinite, the bard says,
but I have never known

the sea, as I never could
know you, quick &

eyebright as a grackle who
snared the love of my love

as if it were simple & bounded
as a ring spied in the grass.

Oh, I take you, nonetheless,
mystery you are, fragments

of a tale told enough to
make the telling common,

though the story be
untouchable. I take you,

alongside mine, remembering
a girlchild turned woman

with a babe in the wild—that
at least a familiar yarn spun

fine in the turning, the spindle's
comforting clatter & roll.

Hymn to Distance

Saint Louis, 1814

A fox, I have heard, heeds
the vole moving

through the grass from
one hundred yards off,

hillocked ears open
to the current of sound.

I walk the cobbles & strain
my mark. For what stirrings

am I attuned? Rumble
of the corduroy roads, over

which worn wagons haul
whiskey, flour, sage, &, I pray,

cloth thicker than muslin.
Or the slow bricking in

of hinterland & hollow?
The mew of a child—mine,

yes, or the hushed ghosts
wandering field & prairie,

which gather at the river,
but are too light, too made

of moongust, to ride the runnel
to headwater or home.

The Coming of the *Zebulon M. Pike*, First Steamboat
to Ascend the Missouri to Saint Louis
1817

A blacksnake big
around as a man's
wrist once ate three
of papa's pullets.
One I watched it
disgorge, slicked
with the phlegm
of the snake's belly
& smooth as the eggs
it was meant to
give us. The other
two nestled there
in the racer's
bulged coil. It fled
from me, fat &
slow, as the smoke
that belches
from the ship's
stacks moves in
the heat, indolent,
inevitable, bulbous
with the tale
of its arrival, with
all the mail & its
bright, round news.
Strange, & slippery,
that word from home
might reach me now
by breath alone.

Teaching Meriwether the Piano
Saint Louis, 1818

Gentle, first of mine. What you
finger has traveled

beyond our gift of reckoning.
Borne on a boat down

the wide & turbid river we know,
rattled on roughhewn roads.

Patience, dear son, much farther
than that: to the home of a beast

we cannot even capture with
our minds, which felt its flesh

rend & fail, & surely cried out
as you have done, as I do, hush now,

in the body's despair. Attend,
as now you draw with your

willow-small hands such stately
music from its brittle teeth.

Dead Reckoning
Saint Louis, 1818

On sleepless nights I check
our children's breath, then

drift to your desk, slide open
the map drawer, & touch

the worn faces. How you love
these lines & keys, each last

known point, seeking distance
& direction over landmark,

tributaries finely etched
as the lines in an old man's

jowl. The quill whose feather
rises to greet my palm rests.

What sense of pace I have
slips off, tracing your inky paths,

rivulets that will outlive me,
all that we might know of

our place having flown from
your hand, conceived somehow

motherless, uncoupled—
child of solitude, study, & star.

On the Cancer

Saint Louis, 1819

I wonder what
from the world
outside the body

it resembles. Egg
yolk, rusted spool,
sycamore's twisted

fingers tucked in
on its own dry fist.
Could its sickness

travel through my
child's mouth, that
dense estuary of pain

current in my milk,
its ache suckled from
my breast & swelling

in the bones of my
babes. I wonder if it
rests, or moves

in the night, trailing
its nickeled thread
of slime through me,

quick, slick chisel
unchinking the body's
cornerstones.

V
Montana

Still Life with Copper Creek & the Unabomber

The name spoke of sharp light
gathered around stones & cast up

against the undersides of aspen
leaves or carried for miles

in a hawk's rusty plumage.
But the place had burned,

& though a few pines
sheltered the brook, all else

was scar & skeleton,
whole swaths of antlered trees

& dust, Snowbank Lake a low
puddle where cutthroat

turned bellyup. The nearest town
was Lincoln, its tiny library

the one in which Kaczynski
made his requests for just

a little-odd interlibrary loans,
though the librarian there

called him polite, quiet,
& where in a clapboard cabin

he tamped his hatred into cold
cylinders. He would claim

that it was development—
a road through wilderness he loved—

that turned his mind to darkness.
How long fire must have been kept

from this place, deadfall & brush
piling, awaiting ignition,

the jackpine & lodgepole dropping
year after year the cones

which require flame to spread
their seeds, to pry open

sap's seal like some fetal fist,
fingers cracking apart

at last, that spreads,
& reaches, & grips.

Anti–Ars Poetica

for Steve Scafidi

There are days the anger
dries it up. There's the sense
that the driver pulled over,

lugged the unicorn into
his pickup, opened the pale
hide with a Buck knife,

fed the red wet flesh
through a slurping grinder
& into neat white packages

with a pleasant heft
& tossed the horn
to the dogs. The sense

that he didn't. & what if
the brown stains on fingertips
& the shapeliness of cedar

planed to silt's smoothness
will not send a child
to college? For most, a man

splitting wood remains
meaningless. What if it all
just means what it means?

Arrow Marks Spot Where His Dash to a Terrible Ending Occurred
—1911 postcard of Cromwell Dixon's last flight from Helena

The photo snares the plane in gray afternoon light:
spiderlike, pale spruce in intricate geometry,

     absurdly airborne, its wheels fit for a child's

wagon. Pilot & cockpit are unseen, hovering
somewhere beyond the engine's growl, moments

     before the plunge. There's no doubt

the field in the photo is the site of the crash, but still,
a tiny arrow, hand-drawn in scratchy black ink

     points to a more specific emptiness

soon to be torn & scorched. But what agency,
what intention, in that word, as if, after crossing

     the Divide, the jagged maw of the Rockies

passed unfed, cottonwoods & aspen dripping
in yellow tongues down damp, sluicing gulches

     & blazing along the edges of the fairground,

as a cold October wind prickled his scalp,
there was only one thing left to do to make

     the moment last: that larking, that prideful—dash.

This Is Your Love Poem, Al

Hand me the priest, you say, & I know enough to pass
you the hard wand which you strike against the fish's face

three times, its slick eyes changing first as if against
the glare of the day's haze of distant fires, late August

& Montana burning, the sun a sore red eye at the end
of the world watching as we bring in the boat & you

open the trout's clean flesh with a knife like a talon,
shirtless in the sun, blood on the brown skin of your belly

& among the freckles from beneath which I fear
a slow sickness tunnels upward like a fat pale fish pulled

toward some perfect hole in the ice in winter's
other world where you will rise from bed naked to stoke

the good embers with old spruce sheltered from the snow
by the cabin's overhang while Orion turns above us

in a long lathe, asking me just as we are falling into sleep
if I will help you clean the chimney in the spring, which

makes me feel as I will come April upon seeing the fox
cubs playing beneath the pine branches, sprung from the den

we had wished all season was theirs & how the joy of it is
ours & not, or like the day coming down from Coffin

Mountain in high summer racing the afternoon storm, but too
late, following your shape through the meadow, wildflowers

alight with rain & you turn your head & close your eyes
for just a moment the way you do when listening to a poem.

A Bird in the Hand

What guilt, to see a bird in a building
& rejoice a moment: vessel of the air
I long to breathe—but caught, desperate,
lunging.   A bird is bound so firmly to place:
color, shape, & cry rooted to homeland
its mind a compass untempted
& undeterred by the passage's beauty.

A bird in the hand is worth, of course,
nothing, & a dead bird is no
bird at all—only plumage, carcass,
icicle bones.   They never cease
to startle me, the red-winged blackbirds
arranged along the roadside's flooded fields,
perched on fenceposts or swinging
from reeds, calling up the scent

of my mother's skin, her thin wrist
passing by my face as she would point—
there's one, just as they raise their dark wings
& flare, & fly, flag for unclaimable country,
        window to the heart of shadow.

Tracing It: On the Death of Meriwether Lewis

Having traced
each line with
goose feathers
in a small fire's
flare, he nearly
lost the journals,
his every map
& line. Without
a trace, they say,
though trace is
another word
for trail. Also,
vanishing. A trace
fossil is not
the thing itself:
footprint, root hole,
feel of the pistol
against his thigh,
the wildness he
could never pin
to parchment, dram-
sized whiskey's space
a glass embraced.

Hatch

In the dream, I am
a broken bird, mired
in dense boughs.
My heartbeat
is everywhere,
electric current
in the hollow wires
that lace my wings.
I must be fusing
earth to air, am made
of copper, a shining
map whose trails
are glittering veins
of ore. This year
I've used a bird
for every metaphor.

Maybe I Should Eat That
(for Lisa Allen Ortiz)

she thinks, upon seeing the poem
she had already noticed that now
her daughter has cut from the pages
of the *New Yorker* & left on the kitchen
table like an offering of thin bread, rice
paper, lemon rind, dried curd, its text
shavings of clove curling, about birds
clustering on humming wires, what they
know, & don't, like these starlings
in my apple tree clattering the twilight.

Maybe I should eat that, she thinks,
but not like in the tale of Witter Bynner
spooning DH Lawrence's ashes into his
morning cuppa, no, like grapefruit, woodsmoke,
lilac, like leaning in to listen, the way jealousy
of a fine poem is delicious, lavender
on the wrist, the mint in my mother's field
that would sprawl forth its scent when hoof
& warm hide stirred through it on the way
to maw grass, passed twice through the belly.

Maybe I should eat that, she thinks,
the way handling wool is satiating
like a slow chew, the work of our muscles
in our own cupped ears, the deep moving
muscle of the world, maybe I should eat
that, maybe taste is the tuner of attention,
attention the mother of kindness, the tongue's
attention cultivating as a garden the frolicking
flora & fauna in the tender cage, the glittering,
set table of our gut around which we gather.

The Air Gun & the Stuffed Pony

at the Virginia Military Institute Museum in Lexington

It may not be his & yet it may—the gun
Lewis carried from Philadelphia
to the Pacific, the one he called

great medicine & set off, smokeless,
pneumatic, sans muzzle flash &
gunpowder cloud, flintlock-free

& firable in rain, to amaze
the natives & which he accidentally
shot through the hat of a passerby,

grazing her temple, before the
expedition had even departed.
It gleams behind glass. Yes, I think

it beautiful, but in the way of true
tools: the tale of its travels,
the hands that touched it. Speaking

of tools, I can't help but wonder how
often they run the vacuum in that
glass case above my head, where

stands Stonewall Jackson's stuffed
pony Little Sorrel, who lived long
after Jackson's death first as a POW,

then a tourist attraction at southern
fairs & rebel reunions, at the end
held up for visitors in his feebleness

by a sling round his belly, till the sling
slipped, Sorrel fell to the floor, & broke
his back. Fortunately you don't need

a horse's bones to stuff him. His
skeleton's ashes lie buried at his
master's feet, while his hide dims

under museum lights, the tufted
hair released in gentle molting,
its decay wholly, holy, despite delay.

Blessed Are Those Who Dwell in Your House

To William Clark, on her deathbed
Fotheringay, Virginia, 1820

Even the sparrow finds a home,
the Lord says, & the swallow a nest
for herself, where she may lay
her young. The fireflies turn up
their lamps, & evening spreads
her blue palms over the valley's
sturdy breasts, where no sickness
grows. I know you ride hard,
but take your rest. Smooth
your mount's sweat-slicked coat.
Your house is all the world,
the endless map of your mind,
& my outline as low as prairie
beneath the quilt. Only promise
you'll keep my bones in this place,
which always was what I called
mine. How far can such a missive
travel in a single dusk? Does it find
you awake in the night, the russet
candle of your hair grown silver
over this slow ending. The light
shines in the darkness, O, my reckless
one, my longknife, my river-giver,
& the darkness comprehends it at last.

A Prayer in Closing

Above us bats sail the river of dark, quick sense
in the night's folding blue robe. O the light, going
down, cradled in the moths' dusty thoraxes

which the bats tuck to their breasts, draw to their teeth.
O the light spools in stacks of hay we pass, mired
in the ponds of fields' greater light. O the light

warms your tongue where you map it to the scars
on my belly which are also full of light, quick
scraps of a thin flame that leap from fuller fire. O

give us this day, we say, give it, & don't stop, opening
our reverent, ravenous eyes, our made-for-greed mouths
from which our echoes fly, unfurling fine spruce wings.

NOTES

The opening epigraph is from Jorge Luis Borges's *A New Refutation of Time*.

"52 Hertz": The singing of the 52 hertz whale was first recorded by navy listening outposts scouting for Russian subs in the late 1980s. Its species is unknown, but its strange song frequency, 52 hertz, suggests that no other whales can hear it, that this herd animal travels alone. As the poem suggests, various theories have been put forth to explain its uniqueness, none confirmed.

A note on Julia: The poems in this book set in the early nineteenth century are written in a voice I have imagined for the real-life person of Julia Hancock, born in 1791 in Fincastle, Virginia (where I also was born and raised), who was married to William Clark at age sixteen. Like me, Julia moved from small-town Appalachia to a place on the edge of what some might call tamed: for her, that was Saint Louis, Missouri, the then edge of settled American territory; for me, it is Montana. I have done my best to adhere to facts, historical events (such as, for example, Clark naming the Judith River in Montana after his child-bride-to-be, though no one called her that, or the appearance of the Great Comet during the New Madrid earthquakes), and what I gleaned from research. Her thoughts and feelings—on technology, on Clark, on her children, on animals, on the breast cancer that killed her in her late twenties—are my own imaginings, my way to think about American expansionism and "progress" through a voice at the margins, but not wholly outside my realm. When I have directly quoted or referenced Lewis or Clark, I have usually relied on Bernard DeVoto's edition of the expedition's journals, though Donald Jackson's *Letters of the Lewis and Clark Expedition*, James Holmberg's *Dear Brother: Letters of William Clark to Jonathan Clark*, and a handful of other books informed my research.

A note on Thomas Jefferson and the mastodon: Jefferson was veritably obsessed with mastodons, collecting their bones and, indeed, instructing Lewis and Clark to look for live ones in the West (extinction science was not yet commonplace). For Jefferson, they held a symbolic meaning about America's strength. For me, in writing this book, they also became haunting symbols—but of the consequence and destructive power of the need to consume and own.

"The Pleasuring Ground" and "Strange Things the Animals Do": These poems owe a debt to my friend Jim Robbins and his knowledge of birds (among many other things), which I have plucked from his brain over coffee and from his book *The Wonder of Birds*. "The Pleasuring Ground" is dedicated to Jim. "Strange Things the Animals Do" also owes thanks to my friends Rick Henry and Beverly Magley, and to the writings of John McPhee, for certain tales of animal strange-doings.

A note on Butte, Montana ("Butte Tango" and "April & the Iron-Eaters"): Once known as the Richest Hill on Earth, high-elevation Butte, Montana, was the site of some of the heaviest and most productive mineral mining in the United States, birthing the western legacy of the Copper Kings. The Berkeley Pit, referenced in these poems, is a mile-wide, nearly 2,000-foot-deep open-pit mine on the upper west slope of town that swallowed whole neighborhoods (largely those of ethnic minorities and workers) as it was cut into the earth over multiple decades. The pit remains a massive eyesore and environmental hazard, slowly filling with highly acidic water from below-ground mine tailings. It is estimated that in 2020, Butte, one of the largest Superfund sites in the country, will need to begin perpetually pumping the pit to avoid groundwater contamination. Migrating birds die on its surface yearly. In the mid-1990s, researchers from nearby Montana Tech found the first examples of extremophiles living in the pit's toxic waters.

ACKNOWLEDGMENTS

Many thanks to the journals where these poems first appeared, sometimes in slightly different forms.

32 Poems: "Completion of the Jackson Ferry Shot Tower," "Hawk Moth"; *The Adroit Journal*: "The Air Gun & the Stuffed Pony"; *AGNI*: "Bringing Home the Bull," "Love Song of the Barred Owl," "Field Clearing, after the Wedding"; *The Arkansas International*: "Chestnut Sabbath"; *Bright Bones: Contemporary Montana Writing*: "In the Divorce, Patricia Got the Mammoth Bone," "On the Cancer"; *Broadsided*: "Science Lesson"; *Crab Creek Review*: "This Is Your Love Poem, Al," "Tracing It: On the Death of Meriwether Lewis"; *Devil's Lake*: "Arrow Marks Spot Where His Dash to a Terrible Ending Occurred"; *The Journal*: "Hiking to Goldbug Hot Springs, I Consider the Discovery of Lewis & Clark's Shitter at Traveler's Rest, Montana"; *Linebreak*: "52 Hertz," "Hymn to Distance"; *Quarterly West*: "Endless Forms Most Beautiful," "Blessed Are Those Who Dwell in Your House"; *Shenandoah*: "The River Where You Forgot My Name," "Bread Alone," "Anti–Ars Poetica," "Leap Year & the New Madrid Earthquakes"; *Southern Humanities Review*: "Unrest: Addressing the Great Comet," "Vultures: Collective Noun," "Butte Tango"; *Sundog Lit*: "A Prayer in Closing," "Hatch," "Winter in Montana: Lewis's List"; *The Swamp*: "Maybe I Should Eat That," "Know You from Adam"; *Terrain.Org*: "April & the Iron-Eaters," "The Valley of a Thousand Haystacks," "The Coming of the Zebulon M. Pike, First Steamboat to Ascend the Missouri to St. Louis"; *TriQuarterly*: "Still Life with Copper Creek & the Unabomber," "Gates of the Mountains," "A Bird in the Hand"; *West Branch*: "At the Farmers Union's Women's Conference in Paradise, Montana," "The Pleasuring Ground, or This Week in Animal News"; *Willow Springs*: "Mastodon."

This was a haunted project; the book that resulted would never have come to be without the support and kindness of a good many folks. I am enormously grateful to the editors at the journals who saw promise in poems from this manuscript, particularly the earliest ones in Julia's voice, and brought them into the world for the first time.

Unlike my first book, *Sweet Husk*, this one was written entirely beyond the comforting arms of a graduate writing program—a much lonelier endeavor. My writing community near and far helped prod me and move these poems along. I am particularly grateful to Aran Donovan and Kimberly Driggers, for the periodical long-distance poem-a-day challenges that were enormously generative for me, and to my Montana/Northwest writing community: Chelsia Rice, Lisa Teberg-Johnson, Loren Graham, Alexandra Teague, Jim Robbins, and Kevin Stewart, who kept me scribbling and hoping with their camaraderie and example.

I am profoundly grateful to the folks at Crab Orchard and Southern Illinois University Press for making *The River Where You Forgot My Name* the book I dreamed of: to Allison Joseph for selecting the manuscript, Jon Tribble for his kind and careful edits, Kristine Priddy for guiding me through the logistics, and the rest of the editorial, design, and publishing team for all their good work.

The women at Perugia Press, which published my first book, continue to be an invaluable community and champions of my work, particularly Rebecca Olander. I am lucky to have their friendship and their cheers at my back.

I would never have dared to call myself a writer, let alone attempt this book, without the unwavering love and encouragement of my family, John, Marilee, Meghan, Kurt. And, of course Alex, who made the West a place to love.